TRAIN YOUR BRAIN

BRAIN BUSTERS

KINGFISHER

KINGFISHER

Published 2010 by Kingfisher
an imprint of Macmillan Children's Books
a division of Macmillan Publishers Limited
20 New Wharf Road, London N1 9RR
Basingstoke and Oxford
Associated companies throughout the world
www.panmacmillan.com

Puzzles created by Susie Brooks and Sandy Ransford
Illustrations by Adrian Barclay

ISBN 978-0-7534-1996-0

Produced for Macmillan Children's Books by Discovery Books Ltd

Copyright © Macmillan Children's Books 2010

1 3 5 7 9 8 6 4 2
1TR/0910/AYL/MOP/60HBC/C

A CIP catalogue record for this book is available from
the British Library.

Printed and bound in the UK by CPI Mackays, Chatham ME5 8TD

This book is produced in association with the Science Museum. Sales of this
product support the Science Museum's exhibitions and programmes.

Internationally recognised as one of the world's leading science centres,
the Science Museum, London, contains more than 10,000 amazing exhibits,
two fantastic simulator rides and the astounding IMAX cinema. Enter a world
of discovery and achievement, where you can see, touch and experience
real objects and icons which have shaped the world we live in today
or visit www.sciencemuseum.org.uk to find out more.

CONTENTS

Introduction	4
How to Use This Book	5
Day 1 Puzzles	6
Day 2 Puzzles	12
Day 3 Puzzles	18
Day 4 Puzzles	24
Day 5 Puzzles	30
Day 6 Puzzles	36
Day 7 Puzzles	42
Double Puzzles Section 1	48
Day 8 Puzzles	70
Day 9 Puzzles	76
Day 10 Puzzles	82
Day 11 Puzzles	88
Day 12 Puzzles	94
Day 13 Puzzles	100
Day 14 Puzzles	106
Double Puzzles Section 2	112
Answers	134
Scoring Table	144

INTRODUCTION

Training your brain might sound like a pretty weird idea, but did you know it's just as important as training your body? Doing physical exercise, such as playing football or tennis, helps to improve your muscle strength, your stamina and your reflexes. In much the same way, some scientists think that doing mental exercises can help you to have a better memory and become better at solving problems. You may even notice more things about the world around you. It's also really important to do these exercises when you're a kid. This is because brains are at their best when they're young. You probably think your brain doesn't start wearing out until you're old, but actually your brain can start slowing down in your twenties! But if you take care to keep your brain speedy and smart now, it's more likely to stay that way as you get older.

This book has five different types of puzzle: memory puzzles, word puzzles, number puzzles, logic puzzles and picture puzzles. All these different puzzles help exercise different bits of your brain. But it's not only these puzzles that will help you to get sharp. Most puzzles will exercise one or more bits of your brain, and even things like simple sums or reading out loud can make a big difference.

If you want to be a real mental athlete, then you need to take care of your body, just like a physical athlete does. Make sure you get enough sleep – you need at least eight hours' sleep a night. You also need to eat and drink well. Some scientists believe that certain foods, such as fish, eggs, nuts, fruit, vegetables and whole-grains, are really brill for your brain. Plenty of water will help you think clearly. Regular exercise will make sure lots of oxygen is getting to your brain. This is important because your brain loves oxygen! Even though it's only two percent of your body weight, it uses 20 percent of the oxygen you breathe in.

So now you know how amazing and important your brain is, are you ready to start on your awesome training? Wake up your brain and bust some puzzles!

HOW TO USE THIS BOOK

All you need to complete this book is a pencil, a clock or watch to time yourself with, and a calculator to work out your score. It's fine to write on the pages. Every puzzle in this book is designed so that you can work out the answer, so you shouldn't have to guess for any of them. Neither should you need to use much general knowledge.

Train Your Brain has fourteen days' worth of puzzles. You get a memory, word, number, logic and picture puzzle to complete each day. When you've done your puzzles for the day, look at the bottom of the pages you've just completed. There, it will tell you which page to turn to for the answers. The answer page will tell you how many points you've scored.

There are also two double-puzzle sections. These are designed so you can compete against a friend, but it's fine to do them on your own as well, for some extra training.

All the puzzles are timed. Look at the top, right-hand corner of each page for this symbol:

Time: 2 minutes

If you can beat that time, you win an extra point! But don't worry if you don't. You will still get the points for correct answers, and it's all good practice. Remember, on the memory pages the time limit refers to how long you have to memorise something, rather than how long you have to write down the answers.

In the table on page 144, you can put in your score for each puzzle on each day. The score for each puzzle is out of five, including the point for meeting the time limit. You should also add up your daily score and enter that. It will be out of 25. Be careful to write one in daily, and watch your score soar!

DAY 1

GRID GRIPPER

Take a look at each of these grids for five seconds. Then cover it up and see if you can fill in the same black squares on the empty grid next to it. Then try the next one. No cheating!

Check the scores on p134

JOKE
Q. What do you get if you stare at these grids for too long?
A. Square eyes!

BODY BUNGLE

Some of these words might make sense already, but can you rearrange them to spell the names of parts of your body? For example, EARTH can be rearranged to read HEART. TO TOMB is a muddled-up way of writing BOTTOM!

1) RAM _____
2) CAFE _____
3) KEEN _____
4) ANELK _____
5) BELOW _____
6) HURDLESO _____

These body parts are written in mirror writing. See if you can read them without a mirror!

7) NECK _____
8) THIGH _____
9) MOUTH _____
10) FINGER _____
10) STOMACH _____
12) BACKBONE _____

Check the answers on p134

JOKE
Q. If you sit down you have it. If you stand up you don't. What is it?
A. *Your lap!*

MAGIC SHAPES

The triangle on the left is magic! Why? Because the numbers on each of the three sides add up to ten. Can you rearrange the same numbers on the blank triangle, so that each side adds up to 12 instead?

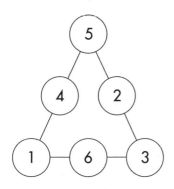
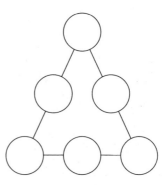

Now try rearranging the numbers in this magic square so that each side adds up to 14 instead of 12.

Check the answers on p134

JOKE
Q. What did the triangle say to the square?
A. You're missing the point!

POOL PUZZLER

Four friends are going swimming. From the clues below,
can you work out who swims what distance and which
piece of kit belongs to which child?

Flippers

Armbands

Kate swims twice as far as Amrit.
The float is Sam's.
The person with the flippers swims furthest.
Amrit swims further than Sam.
Kate wears goggles.

Goggles

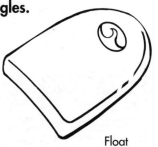

Float

	50m	100m	200m	300m	Kit
Sam					
Jim					
Amrit					
Kate					

Check the answers on p134

PATCHWORK PUZZLE

Samantha Sew-and-sew is making a patchwork quilt from pieces of old fabric she found in a box in the attic. Look carefully at it and answer the following questions.

1) How many stars are there in the quilt? _____
2) How many whole circles can you see that don't overlap with another circle? _____
3) How many triangles are there? Remember to count the ones created by shapes overlapping. _____
4) Are there more stars inside circles, or outside circles?
   _____

Check the answers on p134

DAY 2

SAUCY SECRET

Chef Silencio thinks the secret to his special sauce is safe because no one can remember all the ingredients! Can you? Spend one minute looking at what's in the bottle. Then cover it up and see if you can list them all.

List the ingredients here!

water
pepper
salt
vinegar
sugar
tomatoes
chilli
mustard
garlic
lemon
cream
bacon
onion
toenails
cornflour

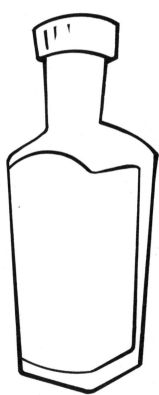

Check the scores on p134

TIP

While you read the list, picture these things in your kitchen – imagine mixing them all up in a pan. It might help you remember!

WHO'S HIDING?

Each of these sentences has the name of an animal hidden in it. For example, if the sentence read: 'In South America they went to Peru', the animal would be 'cat'. See if you can find all the other animals!

1) I did as the rabbi told me. _____
2) Was that Ali on the phone? _____
3) Ellie tried to explain in her bad German. _____
4) I've got terrible toothache. _____
5) Mo used her foot to close the door. _____
6) In the cafe, who got the bigger bill? _____
7) Lia's nail varnish was bright pink to match her lipstick. _____
8) 'Hello,' said Leo. 'Pardon me, but is this the way to the school?' _____

Check the answers on p134

JOKE
Q. Why can't a leopard hide?
A. *Because it's always spotted!*

THREES PLEASE!

Triple-agent Trev has left a secret code in his calendar.
Every time you see a date that divides by the number
three, write down the third letter of his diary entry.
The results should tell you where he's been hiding!

1	2	3	4	5	6	7
Buy disguise	Prepare cover	Encrypt files	Meeting at HQ	Drop dead letter	Trace fingerprints	Ring Moscow
8	**9**	**10**	**11**	**12**	**13**	**14**
Dinner with Tina	Fishing trip	Write report	Order spycam	Search database	Visit library	Check CCTV
15	**16**	**17**	**18**	**19**	**20**	**21**
Submarine training	Watch Bond film	Interview Briggs	Follow McFee	Run marathon	Supermarket shop	Plan ambush
22	**23**	**24**	**25**	**26**	**27**	**28**
Learn French	Talk to boss	Dentist 10am	Bug phone	Mend glasses	Decipher code	Shave beard
29	**30**	**31**				
Ursula's birthday	Train 17.55	Operation complete				

TREV IS HIDING IN _ _ _ _ _ _ _ _ _ _

If you managed that, see if you can crack the prime time
code. Look for dates that are prime numbers – numbers that
divide only by themselves and one. Use the first letter of these
diary entries to uncover Trev's fake name. By the way, one
itself is not a prime number!

_ _ _ _ / _ _ _ _ _ _

Check the answers on p134

Time: 6 minutes

FARM FIDDLE

Farmer Florence has divided her land among the crops and animals below. Can you discover what belongs in which field?

Cows are in field ___   Wheat is in field ___
Sheep are in field ___   Barley is in field ___
Pigs are in field ___   Turnips are in field ___

**There are no animals next to the farmhouse.
The wheat is the biggest field of crops.
The cows like to shelter under the trees.
The tractor is kept by the turnip field.
The turnips are not next to the pigs.**

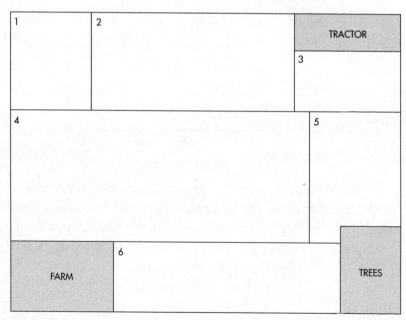

Check the answers on p134

GET YOUR SKATES ON!

Gilly and Johnny are having a great time with their friends at the ice-rink. The two pictures of them may look the same, but they're not! Circle all the differences you can see!

Check the answers on p134

DAY 3

IDENTI-TEST

You see a thief steal an old woman's handbag in the street, but can you remember what the criminal looks like? Take a look at her for two minutes while you cover the identikit below. Then cover the criminal and see if you can pick out her correct features from the identikit.

Hair   Face   Torso   Legs   Feet

Check the scores on p134

SOUNDS THE SAME

Each pair of clues can be answered by a single word.
This word sounds the same but is spelled
differently in each answer.

1 a) The opposite of low

b) A short way of saying hello

2 a) Two of anything

b) A fruit

3 a) Brilliant

b) To shred cheese

4 a) Hang around

b) Heaviness

5 a) The top of a mountain

b) Take a quick look

6 a) An animal you can ride

b) Having a croaky voice

7 a) A kind of tree

b) The seashore

8 a) A long-eared animal

b) What grows on a human head

Check the answers on p134

JOKE
Knock knock. *Who's there?*
Nose. *Nose who?* Who knows!

TOWER TOTTING

Can you work out the missing numbers in this tower?
Each row of two numbers adds up to the single number
in the block above it. All the numbers in the tower must
add up to 80. Start from the bottom and work up.
The first sum (4+3=7) has been done for you.

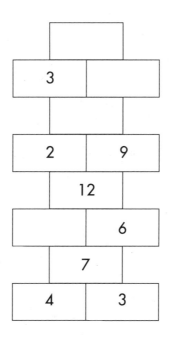

Check the answers on p135

JOKE
Q. What would happen if you took away the 4 at the bottom of the tower?
A. It would topple over!

BIRTHDAY BRAINTEASER

Four lucky girls share a birthday. Each one gets a different present from a different boy. Can you work out who's been buying what for who?

Jess got her present from Max, and it wasn't a handbag.
Tim gave a necklace, but not to Lisa.
Molly did not get the book from Amal.
Leila got a present from Joe, and it wasn't a CD.

	Max	Tim	Joe	Amal	Present
Jess					
Molly					
Lisa					
Leila					

Check the answers on p135

SPOTS BEFORE THE EYES

Susie's Dalmatian dog Dotty has had puppies and below is a picture of them. Below that are four negative images of the picture. Only one negative matches it exactly. Can you spot which one it is?

1.

2.

3.

4.

Check the answers on p135

23

DAY 4

CARD SHARP

Playing cards isn't all about luck! It can also test your brain speed and memory. Take two minutes to look at these players' hands while you cover the questions below. Then cover the pictures and try to answer the questions. Clue – aces score highest in this game!

Nadia   Kash

Jake   Shona

1) Who doesn't have a diamond? _____
2) Who has the highest spade? _____
3) Who has the most kings and queens? _____
4) What four cards does Shona have? _____
5) Nadia has the highest-scoring hand. True or false? _____

Check the scores on p135

Check the scores on p135

JOKE
Q. What would you call Nadia if she had four twos in her hand?
A. The loser!

HOLIDAY CROSSWORD

All the answers in this puzzle are connected with holidays by the sea. The numbers in brackets show the numbers of letters in the answers.

Across

3. Moving your arms and legs to propel yourself through water (8)
6. Military force based on the sea; the dark blue of its uniform (4)
7. Creature you can eat that lives in the sea (4)
9. Another name for the coast (7)
11. I do like to ___ beside the seaside (2)
12. and 17. Two things you use to dig on the beach to make 8. Down (6, 5)
14. We all hope the weather is like this on holiday (5)
15. Small hut or cottage often found near the beach (6)
16. You do this on the beach when you sunbathe (3)
17. See 12 across

Down

1. The place you return to at the end of the holiday (4)
2. Two-piece swimsuit worn by girls and women (6)
4. Ridges of seawater heading for the beach (5)
5. Did you ___ your holiday? (5)
8. Building you can make on the beach with wet sand (10)
10. You may need to go on this if you eat too much on holiday! (4)
11. Close-fitting, pull-on hat for windy weather (6)
12. You use it to play games like cricket and football (4)
13. The remains of the fire when the barbecue's over (5)

Check the answers on p135

CRAZY COUNTDOWN!

5, 4, 3, 2, 1… BLAST OFF? That's for boring astronauts, not brainy ones! Can you work out the countdowns these rockets need to launch? Look at each number sequence and spot the pattern it follows to fill in the gaps.

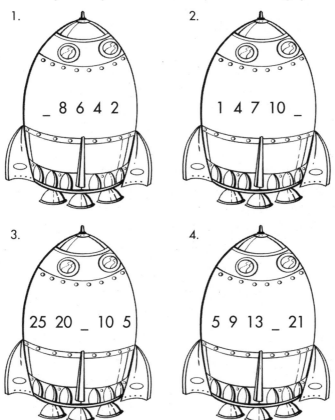

1.

_ 8 6 4 2

2.

1 4 7 10 _

3.

25 20 _ 10 5

4.

5 9 13 _ 21

Check the answers on p135

JOKE
Q. Why is 10 scared of 7?
A. Because 7 ate 9!

DINNER DILEMMA

Six friends go out for dinner. They each order a different dish and they sit alternately boy-girl-boy-girl. Have a look at the menu and clues below, then write down on the table plan who sits where and what they eat.

Steak and chips	£9.50
Sausages and mash	£8.00
Chicken and mushroom pie	£8.50
Meat feast pizza	£7.00
Beef lasagne	£7.50
Spinach and cheese tart	£7.00

Bob orders the most expensive meal and sits next to Julie. Frida is a vegetarian and sits at the head of the table. Jane does not sit next to Henry and she spends £7.00. The person opposite Tom has sausages, which cost more than his own meal.

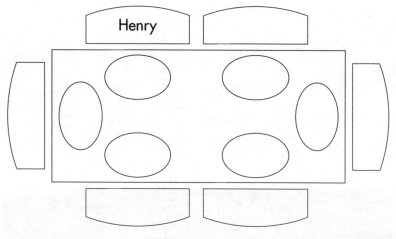

Henry

Check the answers on p135

HIDDEN HATS

It's a blustery day and people's hats have blown off
into the trees. Have a look at the picture and
answer the following questions.

1) How many hats can you spot hidden in the leaves? _____
2) How many people have managed to keep their hats on?

_____

3) There are three lost items that aren't hats.
   What are they? _____
4) How many leaves are flying through the air? _____

Check the answers on p135

DAY 5

FOOD FOR THOUGHT

Spend three minutes looking at the grid below. Then cover it up, try to ignore your tummy rumbling and see if you can answer the questions. Don't cheat by looking at the questions first!

1) How many fairy cakes were there? _____
2) What was in the bottom-left square? _____
3) Which fruit was pictured most often? _____
4) Were there any bananas next to each other? _____
5) What was below the top ice cream? _____

Check the scores on p135

JOKE
Q. Why didn't the two worms go into Noah's ark in an apple?
A. Because everyone had to go in pairs!

MISSING LINKS

Each of these pairs of words can join with another
word to form a new word or phrase. For example,
the words COW . . . . SCOUT can join the word
BOY to form COWBOY and BOY SCOUT.
Can you work out the missing links?

1)	NEWS	_ _ _ _ _	CLIP
2)	EASTER	_ _ _	CUP
3)	HIGH	_ _ _ _ _ _ _	TEACHER
4)	FRONT	_ _ _ _	MAT
5)	NOTE	_ _ _ _	CASE
6)	TORTOISE	_ _ _ _ _	FISH
7)	DAY	_ _ _ _ _	BULB
8)	HOT	_ _ _	COLLAR
9)	SEA	_ _ _ _	WAYS
10)	PINE	_ _ _ _ _	PIE
11)	SHORT	_ _ _ _ _	KNIFE
12)	STEAM	_ _ _ _ _ _	BLADE

Check the answers on p135

SUDOKU SIXER

Fill in the squares of this sudoku puzzle using only the numbers one to six. To get it right, each number must appear only once in any row, column or marked block of six squares.

Here's a filled-in puzzle as an example.

3	2	1	5	4	6
4	1	3	6	2	5
6	5	2	4	3	1
5	4	6	3	1	2
1	3	5	2	6	4
2	6	4	1	5	3

					1
2	3				
		5	6		3
1		4			
	6			5	4
			3		2

Check the answers on p135

HACKED OFF

A criminal has hacked into Detective Deepak's laptop and given it a virus (don't ask me how – that's for computer brainies). Each letter on his screen has turned into a different number! Can you write the correct numbers into Deepak's keyboard and work out what he was typing?

CLUE: Deepak can remember the heading on his screen was **MY QUIZ ANSWERS.**

26 6	**1 7 8 20**	**11 25 12 2 3 4 12**

14	9	9	5	24	11	19	19	_____
5	3	25	25	8	12			_____
22	4	8	22	18	3	5		_____
12	2	8	26	26	8	25	15	_____
8	22	3	16	9	22	18	3 6	_____
9	19	6	26	10	8	22	12	_____

Q	W	E	R	T	Y	U	I	O	P
	A	S	D	F	G	H	J	K	L
		Z	X	C	V	B	N	M	

Check the answers on p136

JOKE
Q. What do computer hackers most like to eat?
A. Micro-chips!

WHAT'S MISSING?

These pictures may all look the same, but one item
(a different one each time) is missing from each.
Can you spot what they are?

1.

2.

3.

4.

Check the answers on p136

DAY 6

TREASURE TEST

Treasure ahoy! Captain Jim Jackdaw has struck gold.
Take a look in the chest he's about to haul onto his pirate ship.
After one minute, cover it up and write down all
the booty you can remember.

jewelled crown   gold bars   silver spoon

crystal watch   bag of coins

lottery ticket   diamond brooch   treasure map

ruby ring

hero's sword

Now write down all the treasure you remember here:

Check the scores on p136

Check the scores on p136

TIP

Concentrate on the pairs of words so that one makes you think of
the other when it comes to remembering them.

THAT'S ODD!

On each line of this puzzle, all the words except one have a letter in common! For instance, in the first line all the words have the letter C, except for "TIME". Can you pick out the odd word in the rest of the lines? Then write down the letter it's missing in the box at the end. What do you spell?

CLOCK, WATCH, TIME, CHIME, TICK | C |

PENCIL, LETTER, ENVELOPE, STAMP, MAIL | |

KEYBOARD, COMPUTER, LAPTOP, SCREEN, TYPE | |

TELEVISION, FILM, VIDEO, DVD, VOLUME | |

HEAD, FACE, NECK, LEG, ARM | |

PLANE, TRAIN, LORRY, CAR, DRIVE | |

SPACE, ROCKET, LAUNCHPAD, COUNTDOWN, BLASTOFF | |

RUN, LEAP, FLAP, FLY, FLOAT | |

SNOW, COLD, STORM, CLOUD, RAIN | |

TIGER, GORILLA, HORSE, PIG, GOOSE | |

HAT, SCARF, GLOVES, BOOTS, SOCKS | |

Check the answers on p136

RIDDLE

Q. Llamas and gorillas like jelly. Cuckoos and crocodiles like ice cream. What do caterpillars like?

STOPPED CLOCK

The cogs in Claudia's cranky clock have stopped.
To get them moving again she needs to work out the
missing numbers. Can you fill them in so that the six numbers
around the edge of every cog add up to 30? You can use the
numbers one to nine many times in the puzzle, but remember,
no number must appear more than once in each cog!

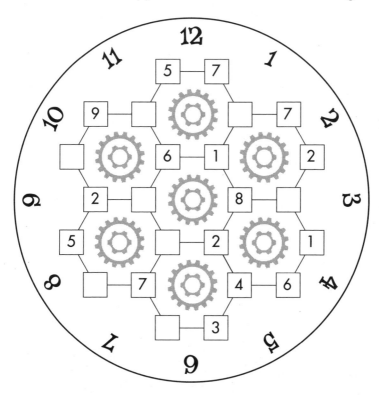

Check the answers on p136

WHATEVER NEXT?

Some inventions have changed the world – and some inventions haven't! At the annual What Were They Thinking Awards, four nutty inventors were competing to be the world's worst. In the end, between them they won the prizes of a wooden spoon, a paper crown, a chocolate medal and a plastic cup. But who invented what, and which prize did they win?

The lead balloon won the wooden spoon.
Y. Knot couldn't eat the prize he won
for his sugar toothbrush.
I. M. Mad walked away with a paper crown on
his head, but not for inventing the
gravy fork (which was Fool's).
U. Fool did not invent the ice kettle –
but he wished he had!

	Invention	Prize
B. Barmy		
I. M. Mad		
Y. Knot		
U. Fool		

Check the answers on p136

ALL SQUARE

Match the numbered squares at the bottom of the
page with those of the main picture. They are not
necessarily drawn the right way up!

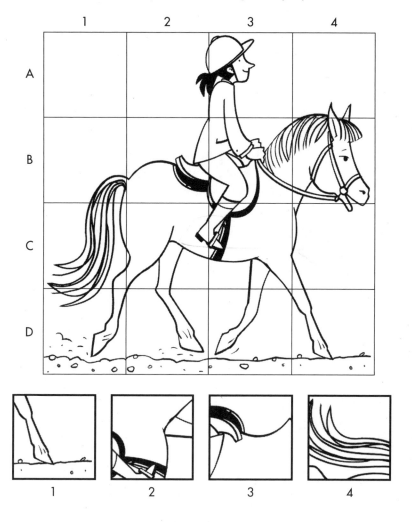

Check the answers on p136

DAY 7

PICKING BONES

Silvia the skeleton is a prize exhibit in Min's Morbid Museum.
But one of the visitors has tampered with some of her bones!
Cover the bottom picture while you look at the top one for
two minutes. Then cover the top one and try to spot
ten things that are missing or changed.

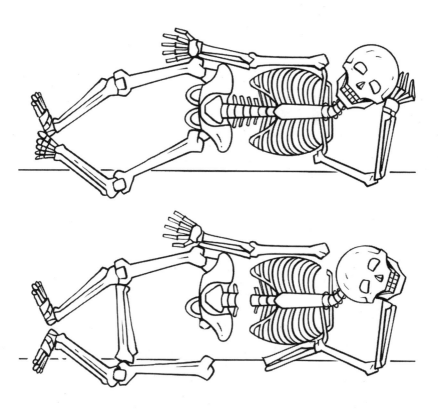

Check the scores on p136

JOKE
Q. Why does Silvia lie around all day?
A. *Because she's a lazy bones!*

JUNGLE JIGSAW

Can you fit the pieces into this jigsaw to reveal the names of the eight creatures listed below? We've put in the first piece to start you off!

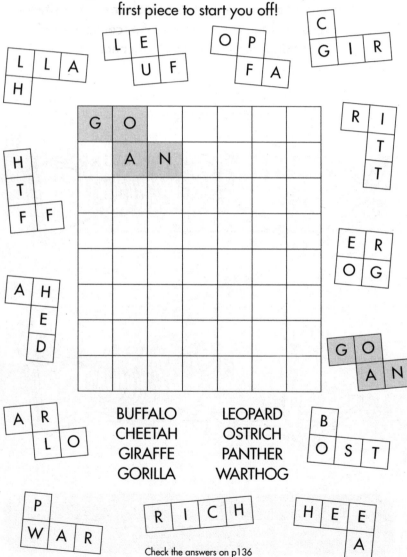

BUFFALO   LEOPARD
CHEETAH   OSTRICH
GIRAFFE   PANTHER
GORILLA   WARTHOG

Check the answers on p136

44

HANDY AT HANJIE?

To solve these Japanese hanjie puzzles, you have to shade squares according to the numbers at the end of each row and column. So a '2' at the top of a column means two touching squares must be shaded in that column. A '5' at the end of a row means all five squares need shading.

	1	2	3	4	5
1					
2					
3					
4					
5					

	1	5	2	1	1
1					
1					
2					
5					
1					

	1	2	5	2	1
5					
3					
1					
1					
1					

This one's filled in to help you!

To make it a bit trickier, we can add extra numbers. So a '2 2' at the end of a row or column means there should be two shaded squares touching, then a gap, then another two. Try these!

		1	2		2	1
		1	2	3	2	1
2	2					
	3					
	1					
	3					
2	2					

						1
		3	3	2	1	3
3	1					
	3					
2	1					
	1					
	2					

Check the answers on p137

CHESS CHASE

These chess pieces are playing a new game.
The knight is racing to his castle and the king to his queen.
They each throw a dice to work out their moves,
as shown in the table below.

Number on dice	Move
1	One step left
2	Two steps right
3	One step forward, two steps left
4	One step forward, one left, two right
5	One step left, three forward
6	Three steps forward, two right, one left

These are the numbers that the knight and king have thrown. Can you work out
what they need to complete their journeys? Don't forget, each time they go left
or right their arrow will turn to point in that direction.

Knight 1, 2, 4, 3, 3, __   King 3, 6, 2, 2, 6, __

Check the answers on p137

ON THE PITCH

Danni is practising her football skills.
Which two pictures of her are exactly the same?

Check the answers on p137

DOUBLE PUZZLES

DOUBLE PUZZLES INTRODUCTION

After a week of hard training, you've reached your first double puzzles section. Now you can show a friend how neat and nifty your brain has become! Just like before, here you have memory, word, number, logic and picture puzzles, but this time they come in pairs – one for you, and one for your friend. Each of the puzzles in a pair is the same level of difficulty, and has the same time limit, so it should be fair. You can do them at the same time, if you can manage not to knock each other's arms, or you can take it in turns and time each other, to see if you both complete the puzzle within the time limit.

If you'd rather, you can do this section on your own. See if you can do the second puzzle in the pair faster than the first! Extra training like this will give you a boost when you start your next day's worth of questions.

Remember not to worry if your friend beats you, or if sometimes you're slower than others. It's all good practice, and it's not a bad thing to have brainy friends!

SPACE VISION

Hold onto your hat... and your breakfast! In space it's hard to pin anything down. Try to remember what's going on in this picture. Then, after two minutes, cover it up and answer the questions below.

1) How many astronauts were awake? _____
2) What was showing on the laptop screen? _____
3) What was one astronaut trying to eat? _____
4) How many toothbrushes did you see? _____
5) What was on the playing card? _____

Check the scores on p137

CRIME SEEN!

Calling all detectives – it's time to investigate a crime scene.
Have a good look at the picture for two minutes. Then cover
it up and see if you can solve the questions below.

1) How many bullet holes were in the cabinet? _____
2) What was in the investigator's pocket? _____
3) What was in the plastic bag? _____
4) What item of clothing had the burglar dropped? _____
5) What was the investigator taking a photo of? _____

Check the scores on p137

WORD WHIZ

The aim of this game is to fill in as many real words as you can in the rows and columns below. With a friend, take it in turns to call out a letter of the alphabet. Both of you must mark that letter in one of the empty squares on your grid. When you've run out of space, add up your scores as shown on the opposite page. The same word can appear more than once and count towards your score each time.

Words can be read up, down or even backwards, as long as they are in a straight line. You're not allowed to use names!

In the grid below you have five words already: TOMATO, TO, MAT, AT, TO (27 points).

T	O	M	A	T	O

LETTER MASTER

Have a read of the rules opposite, but use
this grid, in which you already have the words
RABBIT, BIT, IT and BAR (27 points).

R	A	B	B	I	T

Scoring
6-letter word = 12 points
5-letter word = 10 points
4-letter word = 8 points
3-letter word = 6 points
2-letter word = 3 points

ONE-TUSHIKI

To solve a futushiki puzzle, you don't have to be
Japanese but you do have to follow these rules:

Use only the numbers one to five.
Each number can appear only once in any row or column.
You must pay attention to the arrows:
x>y means x is bigger than y
x<y means y is bigger than x
In other words, the narrow part of the arrow
points towards a smaller number than the wide part.

2	5	4 > 3	1

v   ^   v

1	4	5	2	3

3 > 1	2	5	4

^   ^   ^   ^

4	2	3	1	5

^

5	3 > 1	4	2

Above is one
puzzle filled in
as an example.

3 < ☐ < ☐	☐ > ☐

v   ^

☐	☐	☐	☐ > ☐

v   ^

☐	3 > ☐	☐ > ☐

☐	☐ < ☐	☐	☐

^   v

☐	1	☐ > ☐ > ☐

Check the answers on p137

TWO-TUSHIKI

Look at the rules opposite and off you go!

Check the answers on p137

ZOODOKU

Can you arrange the zoo animals so that there's just one of
each animal in every row, column and marked enclosure?

G=Giraffe   S=Sea-lion
L=Leopard   T=Tiger
P=Panda   Z=Zebra

	G		Z	P	
			P		L
G		Z			S
P			L		G
S		P			
	T	L		G	

Check the answers on p137

TILE TROUBLE

Mary wants to tile her bathroom wall so that no matching tiles are in the same row, column or block of six. How does she do it?

These are the six types of tile Mary has.

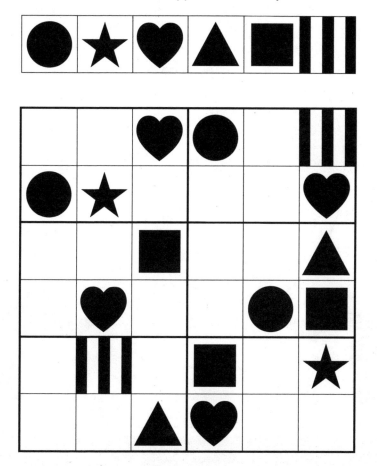

Check the answers on p137

WATER WALLS

There's a big, round pool at Zany's zoo. The zookeeper decides to build two circular walls inside it to separate the five different types of animal. How does she do it? Your walls can overlap.

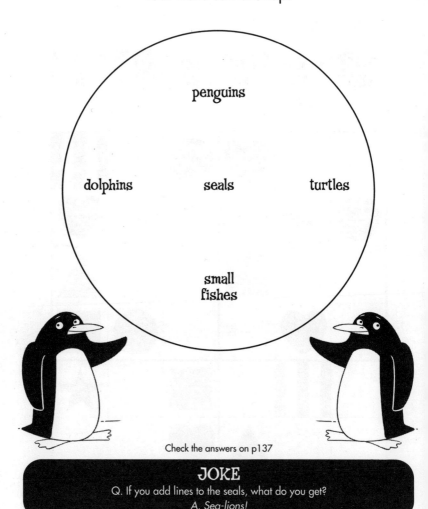

Check the answers on p137

JOKE
Q. If you add lines to the seals, what do you get?
A. *Sea-lions!*

SAFARI SPLIT

Using just three straight lines, can you separate
the safari park into six areas, each containing
one elephant and one mouse?

mouse

elephant

elephant

elephant

mouse

mouse

elephant

elephant

mouse

mouse

mouse

elephant

Check the answers on p138

JOKE

Q. What do you get if you cross an elephant with a mouse?
A. *Extra-big holes in the cheese!*

IT'S PLANE TO SEE

There's a plane flying by, but which is its shadow? Cover the shadows while you look at the picture for one minute. Then cover the picture and decide which shadow is correct.

Check the scores on p138

FULL STEAM AHEAD

Can you spot the steam train's shadow? Cover the shadows while you spend one minute looking at the picture. Then cover the picture and choose which shadow is correct.

1.

2.

3.

4.

Check the scores on p138

JOKE
Q. When is a train not a train?
A. When it turns into a station!

SPELLBOUND

Witless Wanda is in a bit of a fix. Her spellbook has fallen apart and she can't remember what she needs to turn her frog back into a prince. Can you rearrange these pieces in the grid below, to fit her spell back together? If a whole word doesn't fit at the end of a line it starts again at the beginning of the next line. Her cat has put in a few clues to help you.

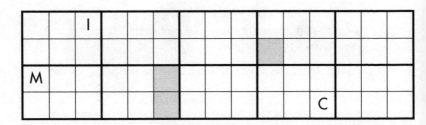

Check the answers on p138

INVISIBLE INK

Now can you mend Wanda's spell that's called
"How to be invisible on Mondays"? The pieces fit into
the grid as explained on the page opposite.

E	A
W	I	T

	B	R
C	H	

R	I	D
D		T

	A	N
O	S	E

O	O	M
A		N

	T	I
R	Y	'

	W	H
	A	

I	N	G
O	E	S

C	K	L
S		T

I	L	E
F	A	I

		T				H					
	W										
											S

Check the answers on p138

63

PONGY PILE UP!

Each of these lorries is carrying the same number of cabbages as the two it is standing on. In other words, you have to add the numbers in two next-door lorries to get the number in the lorry above. Can you fill in the missing numbers?

Check the answers on p138

JOKE

Q. What do you use to fix a hole in a cabbage?

A. A cabbage patch!

TRAIN STACK

Each of these train carriages is transporting the same number of chickens as the two it is standing on. Fill in the missing numbers, as described on the opposite page.

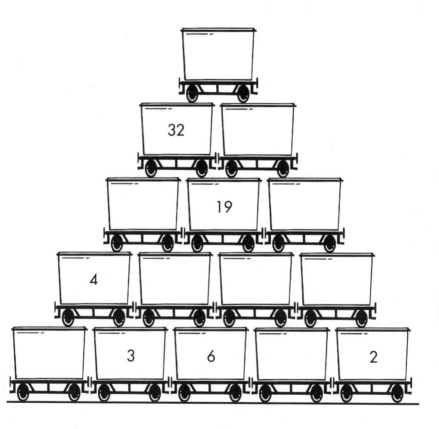

Check the answers on p138

JOKE

Q. Why did the chicken cross the railway track?

A. Because it was nowhere near a road!

CUT THE CAKE!

Here's a birthday double to take on with a friend! Amreeta's cake is square in shape. There's icing all over the top and sides, but none on the bottom. Amreeta has eight candles, evenly spaced around the outside.

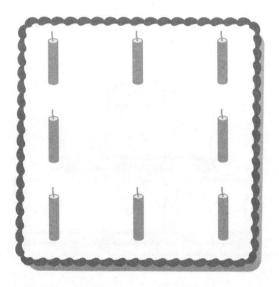

Amreeta's mum marks the top of the cake into nine squares to make nine equal pieces. How many pieces:

1) Don't have a candle on? _____

2) Have icing on one side? _____

3) Have icing on two sides? _____

4) Have icing on three sides? _____

5) Have icing on four sides? _____

Check the answers on p138

PASS THE PARCEL

Luca receives a parcel that's covered differently on all six sides. By looking at the pictures of the parcel, can you answer the questions below?

1) In the first image, what colour is on the bottom of the present?

_____

2) In the last image, what's on the top of the present?

_____

3) What's on the side opposite the black star?

_____

4) What's opposite the grey side?

_____

5) What's opposite the black side?

_____

Check the answers on p138

DO YOU THINK THEY SAURUS?

How many dinosaurs are hiding on this page?
Can you see one that's the odd one out?

Check the answers on p138

SOMETHING FISHY

How many sea creatures are swimming in this tank?
Which is the odd one out?

Check the answers on p138

DAY 8

FASHION FIASCO

Welcome to the fashion show, where things aren't going quite as planned! Cover the bottom half of the page and study the rhyme below for three minutes. Then cover it up and see if you can answer the questions underneath.

Jin is looking jolly in a jacket made by Molly,
While Josh is very posh in a suit he cannot wash.
Take a peek at Sadie, she's in braces for a lady,
And then there's burly Bert who's been made to wear a skirt!
Russell's getting hustled coz he can't do up his buckles,
And little Lulu Short has a button that's got caught.
Lar's behind the scenes sewing patches onto jeans,
But he's running out of time, for it's nearly five to nine!

1) Who made Jin's jacket?

_____

2) Who has a problem with washing his outfit?

_____

3) Who's modelling the braces?

_____

4) What has Lulu Short got caught?

_____

5) What is the time?

_____

Check the scores on p138

IT'S THE OPPOSITE!

Can you fill in the gaps in these sentences with the opposite of the words at the end of each line? If you do, you'll make the sentences true and you might even learn something too!

1) Mount Everest is the _ _ _ _ _ _ _ mountain in the world. LOWEST

2) The world's _ _ _ _ _ _ _ river is the River Nile. SHORTEST

3) Lake Baikal is the _ _ _ _ _ _ _ lake in the world. SHALLOWEST

4) Antarctica is the _ _ _ _ _ _ _ place on earth. HOTTEST

5) The cheetah is the _ _ _ _ _ _ _ animal on land. SLOWEST

6) The _ _ _ _ _ _ _ animal is the blue whale. SMALLEST

7) The elephant is the _ _ _ _ _ _ _ _ land animal. LIGHTEST

8) Howler monkeys are the _ _ _ _ _ _ _ animals in the jungle. QUIETEST

9) Tarantulas have an _ _ _ _ number of legs. ODD

10) The rhinoceros beetle is incredibly _ _ _ _ _ _ for its size. WEAK

11) Strawberries are _ _ _ _ _. BITTER

12) Diamonds are _ _ _ _ _ _ _ _. CHEAP

Check the answers on p138

Check the answers on p138

RIDDLE
Q. What's the opposite of the opposite of the opposite of the opposite of the opposite of the opposite of I remember?

JOKE
Q. What's the longest word in the English language?
A. Smiles (There's a mile between the first and last letters!)

IT ALL ADDS UP!

In the grid below, the numbers in the rows add up to the numbers on the right, and the numbers in the columns add up to the numbers below. Can you fill in the empty grids in different ways, so the sums are still correct? You're not allowed to use zero!

2	3	5
8	1	9
10	4	

		5
		9
10	4	

		5
		9
10	4	

Now try this one, using only the numbers one to nine. There are two variations!

		15
		12
10	17	

		15
		12
10	17	

Check the answers on p139

JOKE
Q. What three numbers make a bargain?
A. 2-4-1!

QUICKFIRE QUIZ

Read these questions then see if you can answer
them straight away. Don't think too much, use logic!

1) Kerry's mum has four children. The first is called Mandy,
the second is called Sandy, the third is called Candy.
What is the fourth child called?

_____

2) If yesterday's tomorrow was Monday, what day is
three days after tomorrow's yesterday?

_____

3) Two astronauts are looking at a photo album. One is the
brother of the other astronaut's son. How are they related?

_____

4) There are 19 children in Asa's class. All but 11 are boys.
How many girls are there?

_____

Check the answers on p139

MARSH MARCH

Can you find the shortest way across the
swamp without getting your feet wet?

Check the answers on p139

DAY 9

CAULDRON CONUNDRUM

What's Wizard Wonko concocting in his cauldron?
Dare to have a look for one minute, then cover it up before
he pops you in too! Write down all the grisly bits
you can remember in the spaces below.

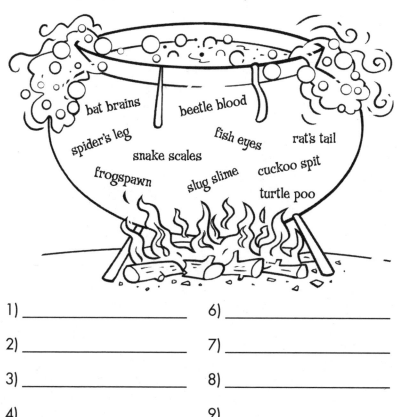

bat brains

beetle blood

spider's leg

fish eyes

rat's tail

snake scales

frogspawn

slug slime

cuckoo spit

turtle poo

1) _____

2) _____

3) _____

4) _____

5) _____

6) _____

7) _____

8) _____

9) _____

10) _____

Check the scores on p139

Check the scores on p139

CHRISTMAS ACROSTIC

Solve the clues and enter the answers in the Christmas tree grid. If you answer them correctly you will find, reading down the column marked with an arrow, the title of a well-known Christmas book.

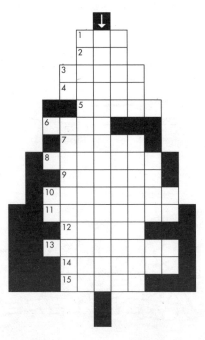

1. Animal that purrs and likes to lie in front of a warm fire (3)
2. Frozen water you can skate on (3)
3. The remains of a roaring fire (5)
4. A gathering of people to celebrate Christmas or other occasions (5)
5. and 6. Pastry treats we eat at Christmas (5, 4).
6. See 5 above
7. Sweet fruits we eat dried at Christmas (5)
8. Means by which Santa enters a house (7)
9. Building in which Jesus is said to have been born (6)
10. We like to give and receive these at Christmas (8)
11. You may hang this up for Santa to fill with clue 10. (8)
12. Santa's second name (5)
13. Small dried fruits in a Christmas cake and Christmas pudding (8)
14. You may have fun making one of these in the snow (7)
15. Prickly evergreen tree whose branches we put in the house at Christmas (5)

Check the answers on p139

SPEED SUMS

See how quickly you can race through these number puzzlers.

1) Seven children are in a race. Tamara is behind Sanil, who is three places in front of the person in sixth place. What position is Tamara in when she has overtaken Sanil?

_____

2) Johnnie collects toy cars. For Christmas he is given £20. In the toy shop, the cheapest cars are £2 while others cost £5 and £7. Johnnie buys four cars and gets £1 change. How many of each price does he buy?

_____

3) Zoe and Sara have 16 cousins between them. Sara has three times as many cousins as Zoe. How many cousins does each girl have?

_____

4) Rachel rollerblades at a speed of ten kilometres per hour. Her dad drives one kilometre in a minute. How many times could her dad drive ten kilometres while Rachel rollerbladed the same distance?

_____

Check the answers on p139

FUSSY FLOWERBED

Geeta is very fussy about where she plants her flowers.
From the clues below, can you fill in the missing
flowers in the flowerbed?

She doesn't want poppies next to bluebells.
Bluebells should not be next to daffodils either.
Daffodils should not be next to sweet peas.
Sweets peas should be kept away from roses too.
Lilies must not go near the roses.
Irises and lilies must be kept apart.
Foxgloves can't be near the edge of the bed,
or near the irises.
Sweet peas should be next to irises.

Here's the flowerbed. IMPORTANT: If flowers touch
diagonally, that counts as being next to each other!

	Lilies	
Poppies		

Check the answers on p139

PASTA PROBLEM!

Which two people are eating the same piece of spaghetti?

Jorg

Sonia

Cassia

Oscar

Check the answers on p139

DAY 10

WEATHER WARNING

All weathers are coming to Brainyland! You can see the forecast on Mr Met-Reader's map. But when the map is hidden, will you remember where you'll need your umbrella? Study the map for two minutes. Then cover it up and see if you can draw the symbols in the right place on the outline map below.

Check the scores on p139

JOKE
Q. What can you push up a drainpipe down but not pull down a drainpipe up?
A. An umbrella!

GOING BATTY

To solve these batty brainteasers, you need to use your imagination. Think about how the words or numbers are written, what position they are in and how they sound. Try to work out a word or phrase from each.
We've done the first one for you.

ꓘƆAꟼ = BACKPACK

1) L
  I
E

_____

2) D
  N
  A
  T
  S

_____

3) (MERRYGO)

_____

4) **SECRET** ⟵
SECRET
SECRET

_____

        5
5) 1 2 3 4 6 7 8

_____

6) PIGGY
(**PIGGY**)
PIGGY

_____

Now try a couple with pictures too!

7)

_____

8) T 🌧 Y 🥄 B 🌧

_____

A MAZE'N MATHS!

Can you make your way through the maze by adding five to each number you meet? But there's a twist! Whenever you land on a grey square, you must divide the number by two instead. We've put in a few arrows to start you off.

START 1 ↓	13	8	4	9	7
6 →	11→	16 ↑	2	30	34
15	13	21	7	12	17
20	14	19	11	6	25
27	24	15	8	3	18
7	23	18	13	30	14
16	28	9	12	17	22
20	19	14	7	18	11 FINISH

Check the answers on p140

Time: 3 minutes

WHOSE CLUES?

A robber is on the run – but who spotted him where,
and what was each person's clue?

**The footprint was found in a lion dropping at the circus.
Vashti was inspecting mummies at the museum
when she found her clue.
Eagle-eared Euan heard a phone ringing, but not at the fair.
Graham picked up a hair that had fallen into his drink.
The thread clue wasn't found at the concert.**

	Circus	Concert	Fair	Museum	Clue
Vashti					
Euan					
Graham					
Steph					

Check the answers on p140

PARTY TIME

The Smiths and the Joneses are all together for a big family party. If the Smiths are all tall, plump and fair-haired, and the Joneses are all short, thin and dark-haired, how many Smiths and how many Joneses are in the picture?

Smiths: _____   Joneses: _____

Check the answers on p140

DAY 11

PAIR'S FAIR

The grid below contains eight matching pairs. Look at it for one minute, covering the grid below, then cover it up and see if you can fill in the missing symbols on the grid underneath.

Check the scores on p140

JOKE
Q. What are you if you get all these right?
A. Pair-fect!

STEPPING STONES

By changing one letter at a time, change the first word to the last in the number of moves shown. Each step must make a proper word. For example, POT can be changed to TEA in three moves, like this:

POT
PET
PEA
TEA

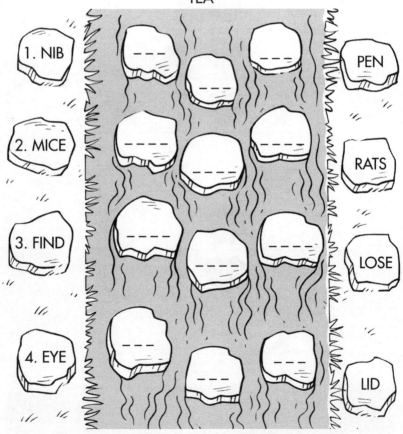

1. NIB — PEN

2. MICE — RATS

3. FIND — LOSE

4. EYE — LID

Check the answers on p140

FUTUSHIKI FUN

Fill in this puzzle with the numbers one to four.
No number can appear more than once in any row
or column. You also have to follow these symbols: < and >.
The symbol < means that the left number is smaller than
the right, for instance 1<2. The symbol > means
the opposite, so 2>1.

2			>
	4	1	v
v			
	>	<	
4	<		

Check the answers on p140

STUNT SQUARES

Can you find the shortest way for the stunt man to get round his track? Draw a loop through the squares, making sure you visit all the hoops and cones. Just remember the following:

At a CONE, the stunt man must turn and go straight for at least one whole square either side. At a FIRE HOOP, he must go straight through, but he must make a turn in either the square before the hoop, or the square after, or in both. He may not go into any square more than once.

Here's how he managed the last track.

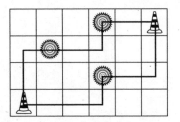

Now can you get him round this one? Start at GO.
WARNING: The blacked-out islands are out of bounds!

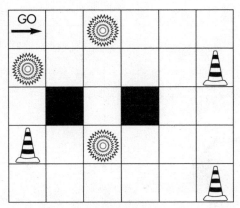

Check the answers on p140

SPACE INVADERS

A Martian has three eyes, two noses, one mouth, three ears, and wears a helmet with an M-shaped aerial on it, a tunic with zig-zag stripes running from his right shoulder to his left hip, a belt with a laser gun in it and black knee-length boots. How many of the space invaders in the picture come from Mars?

Check the answers on p140

DAY 12

POSTIE PROBLEM

It's a tough job being a postman when it's raining!
Pete's postbag is soaked through, and the ink has run on half
of the envelopes he's delivering. Could you remember who
lives where? Study the map of Soggy Street for two minutes,
then cover it up and try to fill in the washed-off words
and numbers on the envelopes below.

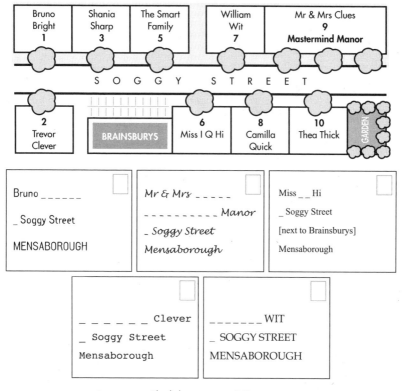

Check the scores on p141

RIDDLE

Q. Poor Postie Pete gets bitten by a bulldog in the
only house that has a garden. Whose is it?

FLYING COLOURS

All the colours listed below can be traced out in the grid. The words may read across, up, down or diagonally, either forwards or backwards, but they are all in straight lines. Letters may be used in more than one word. When you have traced out all the words, you will find that the left-over letters, read from left to right down the grid, spell out three more colours.

A	E	M	A	E	R	C	M	E	R	N
Z	Q	A	L	A	R	O	C	A	O	W
U	E	U	L	B	L	R	H	M	D	O
R	M	V	A	A	I	E	E	C	L	R
E	Y	E	E	M	R	L	R	A	A	B
T	V	O	S	A	A	P	R	L	V	Y
A	A	O	I	G	E	R	Y	I	E	O
L	N	R	O	E	T	U	I	L	N	R
O	E	A	U	N	I	P	L	N	D	E
C	E	N	Q	T	H	O	W	L	E	V
O	R	G	R	A	W	A	O	N	R	L
H	G	E	U	P	F	G	R	E	Y	I
C	I	N	T	E	L	O	I	V	K	S

AQUAMARINE	CREAM	LEMON	SILVER
AZURE	CRIMSON	LILAC	TURQUOISE
BLUE	FAWN	MAGENTA	VIOLET
BROWN	GOLD	MAUVE	YELLOW
CHERRY	GREEN	NAVY	WHITE
CHOCOLATE	GREY	ORANGE	
CORAL	LAVENDER	PURPLE	

Check the answers on p141

JOKE
Q. What's a horse's favourite shade of blue?
A. NEIGH-vy!

HITOR-MISS?

Much like other types of Japanese number puzzle, hitori is about avoiding repeated numbers. The difference is, you have to knock them out instead of writing them in! To play:

Get ready with a pencil to do the knocking out.
The aim is to colour in squares so that no number appears more than once in any row or column.

Here's an example:

1	2	1	3
3	3	1	4
2	4	3	2
4	1	2	1

BUT
You can't colour in two squares that are next to, above or below each other. They can touch diagonally – that's fine. The unshaded squares must be joined to other unshaded squares by at least one side, top or bottom.

Now you try!

2	2	3
3	2	1
1	2	2

4	3	1	2
4	3	2	3
1	2	3	4
1	1	4	3

Check the answers on p141

JOKE
Q. How do you get rid of the number one?
A. Add the letter g and it will be gone!

ARCTIC ANTICS

Ingrid the Intrepid is trudging back from the North Pole. On her way, she buried some spare socks and chocolate under the snow. Trouble is, she can't remember where she put them! Can you crack the code to pinpoint her secret hiding place?

In the footprints around this page, two letters appear only once. Find out which they are, then use them to follow the grid-lines on the map and lead you to the right square. "Z" is not one of them. "Z" doesn't appear even once.

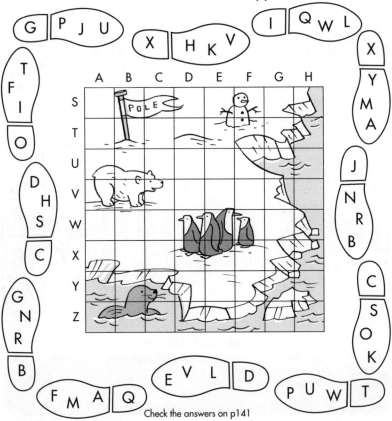

Check the answers on p141

ODD ONE OUT

One of these pictures is different from all the others.
Can you spot which it is?

Check the answers on p141

DAY 13

WHAT A WHIRLWIND!

Lauren's house has been hit by a tornado and all her things
are whirling through the sky! Take a look at the picture
for two minutes. Then cover it up and see if you
can write down everything she's lost.

ANSWERS

1. _____
2. _____
3. _____
4. _____
5. _____
6. _____
7. _____
8. _____
9. _____
10. _____

Check the scores on p141

TIP
Can you imagine these things in rooms in your house? Try it when you read the
list and then see if you can conjure up a picture in your memory.

WORD RINGS

Each of the rings below is made from a word spelled out letter by letter. The words may be read clockwise or anti-clockwise, but they all have something in common. Can you work out what they are?

1.
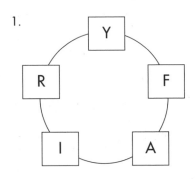

2.
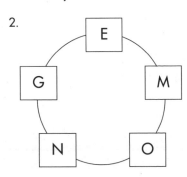

3.
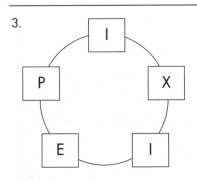

4.
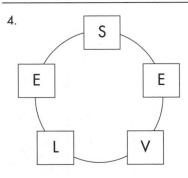

Check the answers on p141

SUDOKU NINER

This sudoku puzzle is similar to the one on page 33,
but this time you use the numbers one to nine.
Make sure each number appears just once
in every row, column and block.

3		5		8	2	6		
2		6	4					5
	7	8		5		3		2
5			1	4				6
1		2		9				4
	3			2		1	5	9
8	5				9		7	3
	4	7			8		2	
9	2			1	4	5		

Check the answers on p141

RIDDLE
Q. How many numbers can you put in an empty sudoku grid?

FIDDLY FINGERPRINTS

After a botched bank robbery, Chief Detective Hugh Dunnit finds a set of fingerprints! He needs to match them to one of his suspects, but in the forensic lab the results are muddled up.

In each of the reports below, **only one sentence is true**. Can you work out who committed the crime? Remember, the fingerprints can only belong to one person.

We'll help you with the first report.

1) The fingerprints were Jed's.
2) The fingerprints were not Lucy's.

If 1 is true, then 2 must be false. That would mean the fingerprints were Jed's AND they were Lucy's. That can't be right, because that would mean both sentences are true!

So it must be the other way round – 2 is true and 1 is false. That means, the fingerprints were not Lucy's and they were not Jed's either.

Use this evidence to carry on with the puzzle:

3) The fingerprints were Lucy's.
4) The fingerprints were not Mo's.

5) The fingerprints were not Jaya's.
6) The fingerprints were not Cal's.

7) The fingerprints were Jed's.
8) The fingerprints were Cal's.

Check the answers on p141

IN SILHOUETTE

Which of these pictures is the one shown in silhouette?

Check the answers on p141

DAY 14

SPIES IN DISGUISE

What's underneath a spy's disguise? Cover the bottom figures for two minutes while you look at the top ones. Then cover the top pictures, look at the bottom ones and see if you can list which parts of the disguises have disappeared before your eyes!

Check the scores on p141

TNG TWSTRS

Doctor Dallio's patient has a rare complaint. He can't say his vowels! Vowels are the letters A, E, I, O and U. They are missing from the lines below. Try reading them without tripping over your tongue!

Now can you put the vowels back in to form some traditional tongue twisters?

1) RD LRRY, YLLW LRRY

_____

2) SH SLLS SSHLLS N TH SSHR

_____

3) RND TH RGGD RCK TH RGGD RSCL RN

_____

4) PTR PPR PCKD PCK F PCKLD PPPRS

_____

If you take the vowels from this tongue twister and put them in order in the following one, what do you get?

I THINK I THOUGHT OF THANKING THEM THOROUGHLY

5) W_SH F_SH D_SH F_R H_NGRY H_G, GN_W_NG B_DS _F B_GGY B_GS

_____

Can you think of three three-letter words beginning with 's' that don't contain any vowels at all? Try reading them in a row very fast!

6) S _ _   7) S _ _   8) S _ _

Check the answers on p141

SYMBOL SUMS

Each symbol in this set of sums is equal to a certain number.
Can you work out what the numbers are and
solve the three sums at the end?

1) ⬤ + ★ + ✚ + ★ + ⬤ = 22

2) ★ + ★ + ⬤ + ★ + ★ = 13

3) ✚ + ☾ + ★ + ⬤ + ✚ = 29

4) ★ + ★ + ★ + ★ + ★ = 10

5) ♥ + ✚ + ☾ + ⬤ + ⬤ = 28

6) ♥ + ♥ + ☾ + ⬤ + ★ = 2__

7) ⬤ + ⬤ + ⬤ + ⬤ + __ = 25

8) ★ + ♥ + ⬤ + ✚ + ☾ = __

Check the answers on p141

MP3 MYSTERY

Four MP3 players have been left behind in the classroom.
Can you figure out which one belongs to who,
and how many songs there are on each?

**Amil has more songs than Tessa,
who has more songs than Jack.
The silver player has exactly half as many songs
as the red player, neither of which are Bella's.
The white player (not Bella's either) has the most songs.
Tessa's player isn't black.**

	50 songs	100 songs	300 songs	500 songs	Colour
Amil					
Tessa					
Jack					
Bella					

Check the answers on p142

IT'S A FAKE!

One of these banknotes is a real one from Witland.
The other is a fake! Can you spot eight
differences between the two?

Check the answers on p142

RIDDLE

Q. On the real note, the Witland symbol looks the same
if you view it in a mirror. Which is the fake?

DOUBLE
PUZZLES

DOUBLE PUZZLES AGAIN!

Here's another double puzzle section for you to do with a friend! Now you can see how much your brain's improved since you last played against each other. Remember, it's fine to do this section alone, as well. That way, each time you do a pair of puzzles you can see whether you're faster on the second puzzle than the first!

FACT
Did you know your brain contains over 160,000 kilometres of blood vessels? Laid out in a line, they would stretch around the Earth four times!

SHIP SHAPE

We are sailing…almost! There's a piece missing in this puzzle. Cover the shapes below and spend one minute looking at the picture. Then cover the picture and pick the shape that goes in the missing hole!

1.   2.   3.   4.

Check the scores on p142

JOKE
Q. What lies on the bottom of the ocean and shakes?
A. A quivering wreck!

MARINE MOSAIC

Underneath the water there's a submarine lurking.
But can you find the missing piece of the mosaic?
Cover the shapes below and look at the picture for one
minute. Then cover the picture and choose the right piece!

1.　　　2.　　　3.　　　4.

Check the scores on p142

DINO DANCE

Can you fill in this chain to find 12 dinosaurs dancing head to tail? Their names are listed below. In each case, the last letter of one dinosaur overlaps with the first letter of the next one inside a shaded square. You might need to tip the page to get all the way round. Let's all do the conga…!

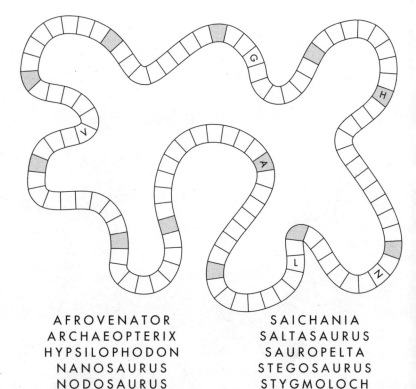

AFROVENATOR
ARCHAEOPTERIX
HYPSILOPHODON
NANOSAURUS
NODOSAURUS
RHABDODON

SAICHANIA
SALTASAURUS
SAUROPELTA
STEGOSAURUS
STYGMOLOCH
XIAOSAURUS

Check the answers on p142

JOKE
Q. Why are four-legged dinosaurs rubbish dancers?
A. Because they have two left feet!

INVENTIBELT

Can you fit the inventions below into the chugging conveyor belt? The last letter of each word overlaps with the first letter of the next one in the shaded squares. We've filled in some letters for you. How quickly can you do the rest?

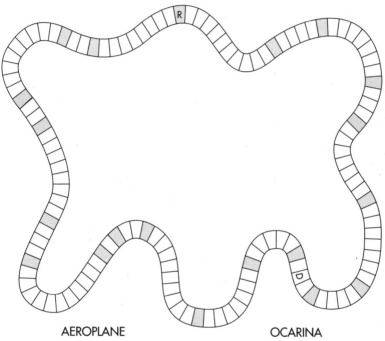

AEROPLANE	OCARINA
BOOMERANG	RADIO
ELECTRICITY	REFRIGERATOR
EMAIL	ROAD
GUITAR	ROBOT
DISHWASHER	ROCKET
LIGHTBULB	ROLLERCOASTER
LOUDSPEAKER	TELEPHONE
NAIL	TELEVISION
OAR	YOYO

Check the answers on p142

KAKURO-UNO

One for me, one for you – can you solve these
double kakuros? Can you beat a friend?

Rules: Columns of white squares must add up to the number
in the grey triangle at the top. Rows must add up to the
number in the grey triangle on the left.
Use any number from one to nine BUT don't use
the same number more than once in any sum.

TIP
Start in the places where there's a single white square
in a row or column. We've put the first number in.

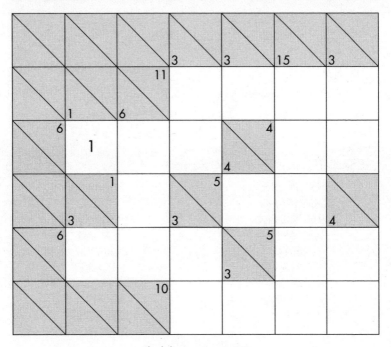

Check the answers on p142

KAKURO-DUO

Another kakuro to solve.
Use the rules shown on the opposite page!

Check the answers on p142

MOVIE MADNESS

Going to the cinema is never straightforward in the Square-Eyes family. They all want to see different things, not to mention buy different snacks. Can you work out everyone's favourite type of film and what they like to eat?

Mum hates musicals but is never sick of popcorn.
Sweet wrappers are always rustling in horror films.
Dad loves nachos (extra spicy) and avoids action movies.
Seeta only likes films that are meant to make her laugh.
Sid doesn't like ice-cream.

	Movie	Snack
Mum		
Dad		
Seeta		
Sid		

Check the answers on p142

SPOOOOKY SENSE

Four friends were exploring a haunted house –
and they found some spooky surprises! Take a deep breath,
try to stop your knees knocking, then read the clues to work
out who met which ghost in which room.

**Ami got spooked in the attic, but not by Floating Felix.
Headless Hal was seen juggling bones in the kitchen.
Robin didn't go into the bedroom, nor did Vampire Vera.
Raina saw Bleeding Bill and heard Ryan
scream from the cellar.**

	Ghost	Room
Ami		
Robin		
Ryan		
Raina		

Check the answers on p142

JOKE
Q. Why was Headless Hal in the kitchen?
A. He was having a coffin break!

MIRROR, MIRROR, ON THE WALL...

Vain Vincente is very confused when he checks his mirror one morning. Eight things in his reflection are not as they should be! Can you spot what they are?

Check the answers on p143

PARK PUZZLE

Gina is surprised by the reflection she sees in the lake in the park, because eight things are wrong. Can you spot what they are?

Check the answers on p143

BAAAAD SHEPHERD

Farmer Florence has lost a sheep! Take one minute to memorise her flock, while keeping the bottom half of the page covered. Then cover the top half of the page and draw the correct markings on to the outline of the missing sheep.

Check the scores on p143

JOKE

Q. How do you call for a lost sheep?

A. Where are ewe?!

PANDA PUZZLE

Zoo-keeper Callum is missing one of his pandas!
Spend one minute memorising the markings of the five
pandas while covering the bottom of the page. Then cover
the top of the page and draw the correct markings
onto the outline of the lost panda.

Check the scores on p143

SPACED OUT

An alien walks into a supermarket, wiggles his antennae
and turns a little greener. How is he going to find
what's on his shopping list when he doesn't
understand the earthling language?

In alien speak, A, E, I, O, U becomes AGGLE, EGGLE,
IGGLE, OGGLE, UGGLE.

Please work out what the alien is buying because
the lady at the counter is confused!

1) BUGGLEN   — — —

2) MIGGLELK   — — — —

3) FIGGLESH   — — — —

4) BAGGLECOGGLEN   — — — — —

5) CHEGGLEEGGLESEGGLE — — — — — —

6) OGGLERAGGLENGEGGLES — — — — — — —

7) CUGGLECUGGLEMBEGGLER — — — — — — — —

Can you help the alien translate the words on these packets into his language?

8) SUGAR   — — — — — — — — — — —

9) CEREAL   — — — — — — — — — — — — — —

10) BISCUITS — — — — — — — — — — — — — — — — —

11) TEABAGS — — — — — — — — — — — — — — — —

12) APPLES   — — — — — — — — — — — — —

Check the answers on p143

BACK TO EARTH?

A earthling lands on Mars. She climbs down her rocket ladder, burns her fingers on the hot metal, then notices that all the creatures on Mars speak backwards, and without any spaces between their words. How does her conversation go?

Martian: OLLEH!

1) _____

Earthling: HELLO! (She's a little slow!)

Martian: EREHGNIODUOYERATAHW?

2) _____

Earthling: SREGNIFYMROFECIEMOSROFGNIKOOL.

3) _____

Martian: TEKCAJROUYEKILI.

4) _____

Earthling: ECIDNIFILLIWEREHWWON?UOYKNAHT.

5) _____

Martian: RETUPMOCATOGUOYEVAH?

6) _____

Earthling: TEKCORYMNIS'TI,SEY.

7) _____

Martian: RABECAPSEHTOTOGNEHT!

8) _____

Check the answers on p143

127

DOUBLE-DOKU

Can you do-doku quicker than your friend?
If there's no one else around, time yourself and try to do the second one in less time than the first!

Fill in the squares with the numbers one to nine, making sure each number appears only once in every row, column and block.

	3	9	4	2			5	
5		7				2		8
			7	5		3	9	
	1	3	8			7	2	5
			5			1	4	
		5	1		3			9
8	5	4		6	7		3	1
7	9	6		1				2
	2		9	8		4	7	

Check the answers on p143

DOUBLE-DOKU-TWO

Race against the clock or someone else
to fill in this sudoku puzzle!

2	5		4		1	3	8	
		6	3	2		5		4
	8	3		7				
		1			3	2		
3		4				8	9	6
5		8	2	4	6			3
	7				2	4	5	
6			7		5	9	3	8
1			8			6	2	

Check the answers on p143

PATTERN PLANS

Vasim is making a map of the fields around his house. Each region of the map has to be filled with a pattern, but no pattern can share a boundary with the same kind of pattern. It's OK if corners of the same pattern touch, though. See if you can complete the map!

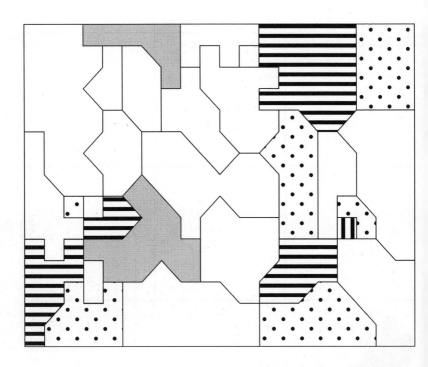

Check the answers on p143

DECORATION IRRITATION

Deedee is trying to decorate her bedroom wall with four different sorts of wallpaper. Each region of her wall has to be filled with a pattern, but no pattern can share a boundary with the same kind of pattern. It's OK if corners of the same pattern touch, though. See if you can work it out!

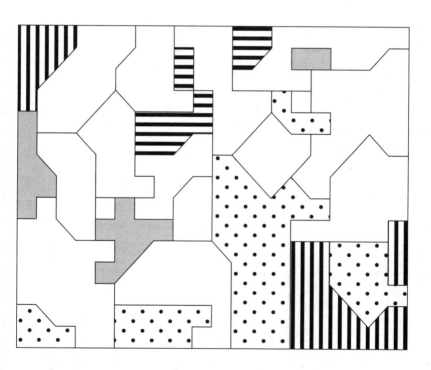

Check the answers on p143

PATCH IT UP!

Someone has thrown something through the back-drop of Joe's theatre! Can you help him select the four pieces needed to patch up the hole? Remember the back-drop is white on the front and black on the back.

Check the answers on p143

HOLY MOLY

A wild animal has jumped through the side of Adina's tent!
Can you help her select the four pieces needed to
patch up the hole? Remember the inside is white,
and the outside is grey.

Check the answers on p143

RIDDLE

Q. What kind of animal do you think it was?

Now here are your answers. Each day's score needs to be out of five, so for many puzzles you have to add up and divide your score. This means you'll probably need a calculator handy.

p7 – Day 1: Memory – GRID GRIPPER
Give yourself one point for each grid you remembered correctly.

p8 – Day 1: Words – BODY BUNGLE
1) ARM 2) FACE 3) KNEE 4) ANKLE 5) ELBOW
6) SHOULDER 7) NECK 8) THIGH 9) MOUTH
10) FINGER 11) STOMACH 12) BACKBONE
Give yourself one point for each question you answered correctly. Now divide by three to get your score out of four. Give yourself an extra point if you did it within the time limit.

p9 – Day 1: Numbers – MAGIC SHAPES

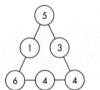

Your answer might be slightly different, but as long as your sides add up to the correct number, give yourself two points for each puzzle you got right. You also get an extra point if you did them within the time limit.

p10 – Day 1: Logic – POOL PUZZLER

	50m	100m	200m	300m	Kit
Sam	X				Float
Jim				X	Flippers
Amrit		X			Armbands
Kate			X		Goggles

Give yourself one point for each distance you got right. Give yourself another point for each piece of kit you got right. Now divide by two to get your score out of four. Remember you get an extra point if you did it within the time limit.

p11 – Day 1: Pictures – PATCHWORK PUZZLE
1) 5 2) 7 3) 11 4) There are more stars outside circles

p13 – Day 2: Memory – SAUCY SECRET
Give yourself one point for every ingredient you remembered. Now divide by three to get your score out of five.

p14 – Day 2: Words – WHO'S HIDING?
1) rabbit 2) lion 3) badger 4) otter 5) mouse 6) gerbil
7) snail 8) leopard
Give yourself one point for each correct answer. Now divide by two to get your score out of four. You get an extra point if you did it within the time limit.

p15 – Day 2: Numbers – THREES PLEASE!
Trev is hiding in CASABLANCA and his fake name is PEDRO VIRTUO.
Give yourself two points for each word you got right. You get another point if you did it within the time limit.

p16 – Day 2: Logic – FARM FIDDLE
Cows: 5 Sheep: 2 Pigs: 1 Wheat: 4 Barley: 6 Turnips: 3
Give yourself one point for each one you got right. Now double it (to get your score out of 12), and then divide it by three, to get your score out of four. You get an extra point if you did it within the time limit.

p17 – Day 2: Pictures – GET YOUR SKATES ON!

Give yourself one point for each difference you spotted. Now divide by two to get your score out of four. Remember you get an extra point for doing it within the time limit.

p19 – Day 3: Memory – IDENTI-TEST
Give yourself one point for each correct bit you selected from the identikit.

p20 – Day 3: Words – SOUNDS THE SAME
1) high/hi 2) pair/pear 3) great/grate 4) wait/weight
5) peak/peek 6) horse/hoarse 7) beech/beach
8) hare/hair
Give yourself one point for each question you got right. Now divide by two to get your score out of four. You get an extra point if you did it within the time limit.

p21 – Day 3: Numbers – TOWER TOTTING

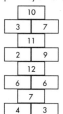

Give yourself one point for each number you filled in correctly. You get an extra point if you did it within the time limit.

p22 – Day 3: Logic – BIRTHDAY BRAINTEASER

	Max	Tim	Joe	Amal	Present
Jess	X				CD
Molly		X			Necklace
Lisa				X	Book
Leila			X		Handbag

Give yourself one point for each present you got right. Give yourself another point for every present-giver you got right. Now divide by two to get your score out of four. Remember you get an extra point if you did it within the time limit.

p23 – Day 3: Pictures – SPOTS BEFORE THE EYES

The correct match is number 3. If you got it right, give yourself four points, plus one more if you did it within the time limit.

p25 – Day 4: Memory – CARD SHARP

1) Jake 2) Nadia 3) Kash 4) 3 ♦ 8 ♥ 7 ♦ 4 ♣
5) true

p26 – Day 4: Words – HOLIDAY CROSSWORD

Give yourself four points if you filled in the grid correctly, plus another one if you did it within the time limit.

p27 – Day 4: Numbers – CRAZY COUNTDOWN!

1) 10, 8, 6, 4, 2 2) 1, 4, 7, 10, 13 3) 25, 20, 15, 10, 5
4) 5, 9, 13, 17, 21
Give yourself a point for each number you filled in correctly, plus one more if you did it within the time limit.

p28 – Day 4: Logic – DINNER DILEMMA

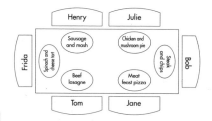

Give yourself a point for each person you placed correctly (you can have the point for Henry, as well!). Give yourself another point for each dish you got right. Now divide by three to get your score out of four. You get another point if you did it within the time limit.

p29 – Day 4: Pictures – HIDDEN HATS

1) 12 2) two 3) two scarves and an umbrella 4) 31
Give yourself one point for each one you got right. You get an extra point if you did it within the time limit.

p31 – Day 5: Memory – FOOD FOR THOUGHT

Give yourself one point for each question you answered correctly.

p32 – Day 5: Words – MISSING LINKS

1) paper 2) egg 3) school 4) door 5) book 6) shell
7) light 8) dog 9) side 10) apple 11) bread 12) roller
Give yourself one point for each correct answer. Now divide by three to get your score out of four. You get an extra point if you did it within the time limit.

p33 – Day 5: Numbers – SUDOKU SIXER

6	5	3	2	4	1
2	3	1	4	6	5
4	1	5	6	2	3
1	2	4	5	3	6
3	6	2	1	5	4
5	4	6	3	1	2

If you filled in the grid correctly, give yourself four points. You get an extra point if you did it within the time limit.

p34 – Day 5: Logic – HACKED OFF

26 6	1 7 8 20	11 25	12 2 3 4 12	
14 9 9	5 24 11 19 19			football
5 3 25	25 8 12			tennis
22 4 8	22 18 3 5			cricket
12 2 8	26 26 8 25 15			swimming
8 22 3	16 9 22 18 3 6			ice hockey
9 19 6	26 10 8 22 12			Olympics

Q 1	W 2	E 3	R 4	T 5	Y 6	U 7	I 8	O 9	P 10
A 11	S 12	D 13	F 14	G 15	H 16	J 17	K 18	L 19	
	Z 20	X 21	C 22	V 23	B 24	N 25	M 26		

Give yourself one point for each line on the screen you translated correctly. Give yourself another point for each letter you translated on the keyboard. Add them together and divide by eight to get your score out of four. You get an extra point if you did it within the time limit.

p35 – Day 5: Pictures – WHAT'S MISSING?
1) crisps 2) sausage roll 3) apple 4) mug
Give yourself one point for each one you got right.
You get an extra point if you did it within the time limit.

p37 – Day 6: Memory – TREASURE TEST
Give yourself one point for every item you remembered.
Now divide by two to get your score out of five.

p38 – Day 6: Words – THAT'S ODD!
The hidden word is CLEVERCLOGS. Give yourself four points if you got it. You get an extra point if you did it within the time limit.
Riddle answer: Jelly. 'Caterpillar' has 2 'l's in it, as do 'llama', 'gorilla' and 'jelly'. 'Ice cream', 'cuckoo' and 'crocodile' each have 2 'c's, but 'caterpillar' has only one.

p39 – Day 6: Numbers – STOPPED CLOCK
Give yourself a point for every number you filled in correctly.
Now divide by two to get your score out of four. You get an extra point if you did it within the time limit.

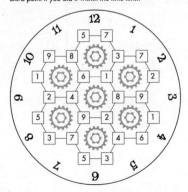

p40 – Day 6: Logic – WHATEVER NEXT?

	Invention	Prize
B. Barmy	Lead balloon	Wooden spoon
I. M. Mad	Ice kettle	Paper crown
Y. Knot	Sugar toothbrush	Plastic cup
U. Fool	Gravy fork	Chocolate medal

Give yourself one point for each invention you got right, and one point for each prize you got right. Now divide by two to get your score out of four. You get an extra point if you did it within the time limit.

p41 – Day 6: Pictures – ALL SQUARE
square 1 – D4   square 2 – C3   square 3 – B2   square 4 – C1
Give yourself one point for each one you got right. You get an extra point if you did it within the time limit.

p43 – Day 7: Memory – PICKING BONES

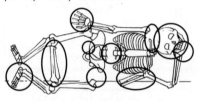

Give yourself a point for each difference you remembered.
Now divide by two to get your score out of five.

p44 – Day 7: Words – JUNGLE JIGSAW

G	O	R	I	L	L	A
P	A	N	T	H	E	R
W	A	R	T	H	O	G
C	H	E	E	T	A	H
G	I	R	A	F	F	E
L	E	O	P	A	R	D
B	U	F	F	A	L	O
O	S	T	R	I	C	H

Give yourself one point for each animal you filled in correctly. Now divide by two to get your score out of four. You get an extra point if you did it within the time limit.

p45 – Day 7: Numbers – HANDY AT HANJIE?

	1	5	2	1	1
1					
1					
2					
5					
1					

	1	2	5	2	1
5					
3					
1					
1					
1					

		1	2		2	1
	1	2	3	2	1	
2 2						
3						
1						
3						
2 2						

						1
	3	3	2	1	3	
3 1						
3						
2 1						
2						

Give yourself a point for each grid you filled in correctly. You get an extra point if you did it within the time limit.

p46 – Day 7: Logic – CHESS CHASE
Knight – 6   King – 5
Give yourself two points for each one you got right. You get an extra point if you did it within the time limit.

p47 – Day 7: Pictures – ON THE PITCH
Pictures 3 and 6 are the same.
Give yourself four points if you got it right. You get an extra point if you did it within the time limit.

DOUBLE PUZZLES
Double puzzles aren't scored like the daily puzzles, but here are the answers for them.

p50 – Double Puzzles: Memory – SPACE VISION
1) three   2) a cat   3) egg and sausages   4) five
5) two of hearts

p51 – Double Puzzles: Memory – CRIME SEEN!
1) four   2) a magnifying glass   3) a mobile phone
4) a scarf   5) a watch

p52 – Double Puzzles: Words – WORD WHIZ
The scoring is on page 53.

p53 – Double Puzzles: Words – LETTER MASTER
The scoring is on the page below the grid.

p54 – Double Puzzles: Numbers – ONE-TUSHIKI

3 <	4 <	5	2 >	1
v			∧	
2	5	1	4 >	3
v		∧		
1	3 >	2	5 >	4
4	2 <	3	1	5
∧			v	
5	1	4 >	3 >	2

p55 – Double Puzzles: Numbers – TWO-TUSHIKI

2 >	1	3 <	4 <	5
		v		v
3 >	2 >	1	5	4
∧				v
5 >	4	2 >	1	3
	∧			v
1	5 >	4 >	3 >	2
		∧		
4	3	5	2	1

p56 – Double Puzzle: Logic – ZOODOKU

L	G	S	Z	P	T
T	S	G	P	Z	L
G	P	Z	T	L	S
P	Z	T	L	S	G
S	L	P	G	T	Z
Z	T	L	S	G	P

p57 – Double Puzzles: Logic – TILE TROUBLE

p58 – Double Puzzles: Pictures – WATER WALLS

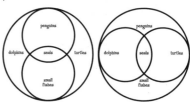

p59 – Double Puzzles: Logic – SAFARI SPLIT

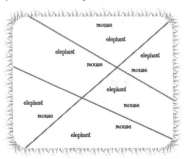

p60 – Double Puzzles: Memory – IT'S PLANE TO SEE
The correct answer is silhouette three.

p61 – Double Puzzles: Memory – FULL STEAM AHEAD
The correct answer is silhouette one.

p62 – Double Puzzles: Words – SPELLBOUND

H	A	I	R		O	F		T	O	A	D		A	N
D		T	I	G	E	R	'	S		Y	A	W	N	
M	I	X	E	D		I	N		T	H	E		H	O
R	N		O	F		A		U	N	I	C	O	R	N

p63 – Double Puzzles: Words – INVISIBLE INK

R	I	D	E		A		B	R	O	O	M		A	N
D		T	W	I	T	C	H		A		N	O	S	E
	W	H	I	L	E		T	I	C	K	L	I	N	G
	A		F	A	I	R	Y	'	S		T	O	E	S

p64 – Double Puzzles: Numbers – PONGY PILE UP!

p65 – Double Puzzles: Numbers – TRAIN STACK

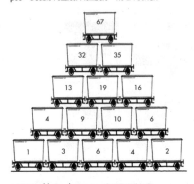

p66 – Double Puzzles: Logic – CUT THE CAKE!
1) one   2) one   3) four   4) four   5) zero

p67 – Double Puzzles: Logic – PASS THE PARCEL
1) black   2) star   3) dots   4) stripes   5) flower

p68 – Double Puzzles: Pictures – DO YOU THINK THEY SAURUS?
There are nine dinosaurs. This one's the odd one out, because there is only one, whereas all the others are in pairs.

p69 – Double Puzzles: Pictures – SOMETHING FISHY
There are 11 sea creatures. This one's the odd one out, because there is only one, whereas all the others are in pairs.

p71 – Day 8: Memory – FASHION FIASCO
1) Molly   2) Josh   3) Sadie   4) a button   5) five to nine
Give yourself one point for each one you got right.

p72 – Day 8: Words – IT'S THE OPPOSITE!
1) highest/tallest   2) longest   3) deepest   4) coldest
5) fastest   6) biggest/largest   7) heaviest   8) loudest
9) even   10) strong   11) sweet   12) expensive
You get one point for each one you got right. Now divide by three to get your score out of four. You get an extra point if you did it within the time limit.
Riddle answer: I remember!

p73 – Day 8: Numbers – IT ALL ADDS UP!

4	1	5
6	3	9
10	4	

3	2	5
7	2	9
10	4	

7	8	15
3	9	12
10	17	

6	9	15
4	8	12
10	17	

Give yourself one point for each grid you filled in correctly. You get an extra point if you did it within the time limit.

p74 – Day 8: Logic – QUICKFIRE QUIZ
1) Kerry   2) Thursday   3) one astronaut is the child of the other   4) 11
Give yourself a point for each question you got right. You get an extra point if you did them within the time limit.

p75 – Day 8: Pictures – MARSH MARCH

Give yourself four points if you found your way through the maze. You get an extra point if you did it within the time limit.

p77 – Day 9: Memory – CAULDRON CONUNDRUM
Give yourself one point for each ingredient you remembered correctly. Now divide by two to get your score out of five.

p78 – Day 9: Words – CHRISTMAS ACROSTIC

	↓					
	¹C	A	T			
	²I	C	E			
³A	S	H	E	S		
⁴P	A	R	T	Y		
	⁵M	I	N	C	E	
⁶P	I	E	S			
	⁷D	A	T	E	S	
⁸C	H	I	M	N	E	Y
	⁹S	T	A	B	L	E
¹⁰P	R	E	S	E	N	T	S
¹¹S	T	O	C	K	I	N	G
	¹²C	L	A	U	S	
¹³C	U	R	R	A	N	T	S
	¹⁴S	N	O	W	M	A	N
¹⁵H	O	L	L	Y		

Give yourself four points if you filled in the grid correctly, and got the title of the Christmas book. You get an extra point if you did it within the time limit.

p79 – Day 9: Numbers – SPEED SUMS
1) third   2) one car at £7, two cars at £5, and one car at £2
3) Zoe: four, Sara: 12   4) six times
You get one point for each question you answered correctly. You also get an extra point if you did it within the time limit.

p80 – Day 9: Logic – FUSSY FLOWERBED

	Sweet peas	Lilies	
Irises	Poppies	Foxgloves	Bluebells
	Daffodils	Roses	

You get a point for each type of flower you put in the right place. You can have the points for poppies and lilies too, even though they were filled in beforehand. Now divide by two to get your score out of four. You get an extra point if you did it within the time limit.

p81 – Day 9: Pictures – PASTA PROBLEM!
Sonia and Oscar
Give yourself four points if you got that right. You get an extra point if you did it within the time limit.

p83 – Day 10: Memory – WEATHER WARNING
Give yourself one point for each symbol you remembered correctly. Now divide by two to get your score out of five.

p84 – Day 10: Words – GOING BATTY
1) lie down   2) stand up   3) merry-go-round   4) top secret
5) high five   6) piggy in the middle   7) eyes in the back of
my/your head   8) train your brain
Give yourself one point for each one you got right. Now
divide by two to get your score out of four. You get an extra
point if you did it within the time limit.

p85 – Day 10: Numbers – A MAZE'N MATHS!

START 1	13	8 ▶	4	9	7
6 ▶	11 ▶	16	2	30	34
15	13	21	7 ◀	12	17
20	14	19	11	6	25
27	24	15	8 ◀	3	18
7	23	18 ◀	13	30	14
16	28	9	12 ▶	17 ▶	22
20	19	14 ◀	7	18	11 FINISH

Give yourself four points if you got through the number
maze correctly. You get an extra point if you did it within
the time limit.

p86 – Day 10: Logic – WHOSE CLUES?

	Circus	Concert	Fair	Museum	Clue
Vashti				X	Thread
Euan		X			Phone ringing
Graham			X		Hair
Steph	X				Footprint

Give yourself one point for each location you got right, and
one point for every clue you got right. Now divide by two to
get your score out of four. You get an extra point if you did it
within the time limit.

p87 – Day 10: Pictures – PARTY TIME
Smiths: nine   Joneses: nine
Give yourself two points for each one you got right. You get
an extra point if you did it within the time limit.

p89 – Day 11: Memory – PAIR'S FAIR
Give yourself five points if you remembered all the symbols
correctly.

p90 – Day 11: Words – STEPPING STONES
1) NIB BIB BIN PIN PEN
NIB FIB FIN PIN PEN
NIB NIP PIP PIN PEN
NIB NIT NET PET PEN
NIB NAB NAN PAN PEN
NIB NUB NUN PUN PEN

2) MICE MITE RITE RATE RATS
MICE RICE RACE RATE RATS
MICE MITE MATE RATE RATS
MICE RICE RITE RATE RATS
MICE MICS MITS MATS RATS
MICE MACE MACS MATS RATS
3) FIND FINE LINE LONE LOSE
4) EYE DYE DIE DID LID
EYE RYE LYE LIE LID
EYE BYE LYE LIE LID
The above are some of the answers you could have given for
each question. As long as you've obeyed the rules, your
answer's correct. Give yourself one point for each one you got
right. You get an extra point if you did it within the time limit.

p91 – Day 11: Numbers – FUTOSHIKI FUN

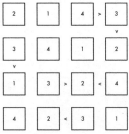

Give yourself one point for each number you filled in
correctly. Now divide by three to get your score out of four.
You get an extra point if you did it within the time limit.

p92 – Day 11: Logic – STUNT SQUARES

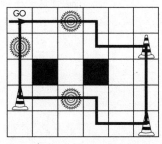

Give yourself four points if you got the answer. You get an
extra point if you did it within the time limit.

p93 – Day 11: Pictures – SPACE INVADERS
Number three and number five are from Mars
Give yourself two points for each one you identified correctly
as a Martian. You get an extra point if you did it within the
time limit.

p95 – Day 12: Memory – POSTIE PROBLEM
1) Bright, 1   2) Clues, Mastermind, 9   3) I Q, 6
4) Trevor, 2   5) William, 7
Give yourself a point for each question you got right.
Riddle answer: Thea Thick's

p96 – Day 12: Words – FLYING COLOURS

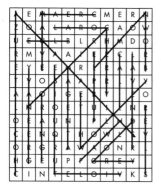

The grid spells out emerald, maroon and pink.
Give yourself four points if you completed the word-search.
You get an extra point if you did it within the time limit.

p97 – Day 12: Number – HITOR-MISS?

2	2	3
3	2	1
1	2	2

4	3	1	2
4	3	2	3
1	2	3	4
1	1	4	3

Give yourself two points for each puzzle you filled in correctly.
You get another point if you did it within the time limit.

p98 – Day 12: Logic – ARCTIC ANTICS
The hiding place is in square Y-E
Give yourself two points for each letter you got right. You get
an extra point if you did it within the time limit.

p99 – Day 12: Pictures – ODD ONE OUT
Picture two
Give yourself four points if you got it right. You get an extra
point if you did it within the time limit.

p101 – Day 13: Memory – WHAT A WHIRLWIND!
Give yourself one point for each item you remembered. Now
divide by two to get your score out of five.

p102 – Day 13: Words – WORD RINGS
1) FAIRY   2) GNOME   3) PIXIE   4) ELVES
Give yourself a point for each one you got right. You get an
extra point if you did it within the time limit.

p103 – Day 13: Numbers – SUDOKU NINER

3	1	5	9	8	2	6	4	7
2	9	6	4	7	3	8	1	5
4	7	8	6	5	1	3	9	2
5	8	9	1	4	7	2	3	6
1	6	2	3	9	5	7	8	4
7	3	4	8	2	6	1	5	9
8	5	1	2	6	9	4	7	3
6	4	7	5	3	8	9	2	1
9	2	3	7	1	4	5	6	8

Give yourself four points if you completed the grid correctly.
You get an extra point if you did it within the time limit.
Riddle answer: One. After that it's not empty!

p104 – Day 13: Logic – FIDDLY FINGERPRINTS
The fingerprints were Cal's
Give yourself four points if you got it right. You get an extra
point if you did it within the time limit.

p105 – Day 13: Pictures – IN SILHOUETTE
Picture three
Give yourself four points if you got it right. You get an extra
point if you did it within the time limit.

p107 – Day 14: Memory – SPIES IN DISGUISE
There are five items of disguise on each spy. Give yourself a
point for each one you remembered. Now divide by two to
get your score out of five.

p108 – Day 14: Words – TNG TWSTRS
1) red lorry, yellow lorry   2) she sells seashells on the
seashore   3) round the rugged rock the ragged rascal ran
4) Peter Piper picked a peck of pickled peppers   5) wish fish
dish for hungry hog, gnawing beds of boggy bugs
6) 7) and 8) any three of the following: sky, sly sty, shy, spy
Give yourself a point for each question you got right. Now
divide by two to get your score out of four. You get an extra
point if you did it within the time limit.

p109 – Day 14: Numbers – SYMBOL SUMS
6) 21   7) ◉   8) 25
Give yourself two points for each one you got right. Now
double your score to get your score out of 12. Now divide by
three to get your score out of four. You get an extra point if
you did it within the time limit.

p110 – Day 14: Logic – MP3 MYSTERY

	50 songs	100 songs	300 songs	500 songs	Colour
Amil				X	White
Tessa		X			Red
Jack	X				Silver
Bella			X		Black

Give yourself one point for each number of songs you got right. Give yourself another point for each colour you got right. Now divide by two to get your score out of four. You get an extra point if you did it within the time limit.

p111 – Day 14: Pictures – IT'S A FAKE!

Give yourself one point for each difference you spotted. Now divide by two to get your score out of four. You get an extra point if you did it within the time limit.
Riddle answer: the bottom note is fake.

DOUBLE PUZZLES
Double puzzles aren't scored like the daily puzzles, but here are the answers for them.

p114 – Double Puzzles: Memory – SHIP SHAPE
Piece two

p115 – Double Puzzles: Memory – MARINE MOSAIC
Piece four

p116 – Double Puzzles: Words – DINO DANCE

p117 – Double Puzzles: Words – INVENTIBELT

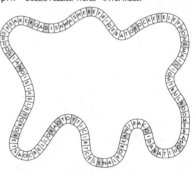

p118 – Double Puzzles: Numbers – KAKURO-UNO

		3	3	15	3
	11 / 6	1	3	5	3
6	1	3	2	4 / 4	3	1
	1 / 3	1	5 / 3	4	1	4
6	3	2	1	5 / 3	2	3
	10	2	3	4	1

p119 – Double Puzzles: Numbers – KAKURO-DUO

	4	15			10	5
4	1	3	1	7	4	3
6	3	2	1	3	1	2
	5	5	3	3	3	4
	3 / 2	1	2	3	2	1
10	2	4	1	3	3 / 3	3

p120 – Double Puzzles: Logic – MOVIE MADNESS

	Movie	Snack
Mum	Action	Popcorn
Dad	Musicals	Nachos (extra spicy)
Seeta	Humour	Ice cream
Sid	Horror	Sweets

p121 – Double Puzzles: Logic – SPOOOOKY SENSE

	Ghost	Room
Ami	Vampire Vera	Attic
Robin	Headless Hal	Kitchen
Ryan	Floating Felix	Cellar
Raina	Bleeding Bill	Bedroom

p122 – Double Puzzles: Pictures – MIRROR, MIRROR, ON THE WALL...

p123 – Double Puzzles: Pictures – PARK PUZZLE

p124 – Double Puzzles: Memory – BAAAAD SHEPHERD
Uncover the top half of the page, and see if you coloured in the missing sheep's markings correctly!

p125 – Double Puzzles: Memory – PANDA PUZZLE
Uncover the top half of the page, and see if you coloured in the missing panda's markings correctly!

p126 – Double Puzzles: Words – SPACED OUT
1) bun   2) milk   3) fish   4) bacon   5) cheese   6) oranges
7) cucumber   8) sugglegaggler   9) cegglereggleagglel
10) bigglescuggleigglets   11) teggleagglebagglegs
12) aggleppleggles

p127 – Double Puzzles: Words – BACK TO EARTH?
1) Hello!   2) What are you doing here?   3) Looking for some ice for my fingers.   4) I like your jacket.   5) Thank you. Now where will I find ice?   6) Have you got a computer?
7) Yes, it's on my rocket.   8) Then go to the space bar!

p128 – Double Puzzles: Numbers – DOUBLE-DOKU

1	3	9	4	2	8	6	5	7
5	4	7	6	3	9	2	1	8
6	8	2	7	5	1	3	9	4
4	1	3	8	9	6	7	2	5
9	6	8	5	7	2	1	4	3
2	7	5	1	4	3	8	6	9
8	5	4	2	6	7	9	3	1
7	9	6	3	1	4	5	8	2
3	2	1	9	8	5	4	7	6

p129 – Double Puzzles: Numbers – DOUBLE-DOKU-TWO

2	5	7	4	6	1	3	8	9
9	1	6	3	2	8	5	7	4
4	8	3	5	7	9	1	6	2
7	6	1	9	8	3	2	4	5
3	2	4	1	5	7	8	9	6
5	9	8	2	4	6	7	1	3
8	7	9	6	3	2	4	5	1
6	4	2	7	1	5	9	3	8
1	3	5	8	9	4	6	2	7

p130 – Double Puzzles: Logic – PATTERN PLANS

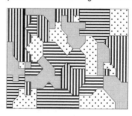

p131 – Double Puzzles: Logic – DECORATION IRRITATION

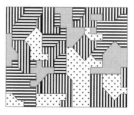

p132 – Double Puzzles: Pictures – PATCH IT UP!
Pieces five, six, nine and ten

p133 – Double Puzzles: Pictures – HOLY MOLY
Pieces one, two, nine and 11
Riddle answer: a rabbit!

WHAT'S YOUR SCORE?

This is where you write in all your scores for the daily puzzles, and add up your total. All the memory puzzles are out of five. You can earn up to four points for your answers on the word, number, logic and picture puzzles, but you get an extra point for doing them within the time limit – so they're out of five too. Add up your scores for all five daily puzzles and put it in the final column, to get your total daily score out of 25.

Don't worry if some days you're better than others, and also don't worry if you're better at one sort of puzzle than another. Everyone has their talent!

	Memory	Words	Numbers	Logic	Pictures	Total
Day 1	/ 5	/ 5	/ 5	/ 5	/ 5	/ 25
Day 2	/ 5	/ 5	/ 5	/ 5	/ 5	/ 25
Day 3	/ 5	/ 5	/ 5	/ 5	/ 5	/ 25
Day 4	/ 5	/ 5	/ 5	/ 5	/ 5	/ 25
Day 5	/ 5	/ 5	/ 5	/ 5	/ 5	/ 25
Day 6	/ 5	/ 5	/ 5	/ 5	/ 5	/ 25
Day 7	/ 5	/ 5	/ 5	/ 5	/ 5	/ 25
Day 8	/ 5	/ 5	/ 5	/ 5	/ 5	/ 25
Day 9	/ 5	/ 5	/ 5	/ 5	/ 5	/ 25
Day 10	/ 5	/ 5	/ 5	/ 5	/ 5	/ 25
Day 11	/ 5	/ 5	/ 5	/ 5	/ 5	/ 25
Day 12	/ 5	/ 5	/ 5	/ 5	/ 5	/ 25
Day 13	/ 5	/ 5	/ 5	/ 5	/ 5	/ 25
Day 14	/ 5	/ 5	/ 5	/ 5	/ 5	/ 25